Who Was
Maya Angelou?

Who Was Maya Angelou?

by Ellen Labrecque

illustrated by Dede Putra

Penguin Workshop

For Sam and Juliet—EL

PENGUIN WORKSHOP
An Imprint of Penguin Random House LLC, New York

Text copyright © 2016 by Ellen Labrecque.
Illustrations copyright © 2016 by Penguin Random House LLC. All rights reserved.
Published by Penguin Workshop, an imprint of Penguin Random House LLC, New York.
PENGUIN and PENGUIN WORKSHOP are trademarks of Penguin Books Ltd.
WHO HQ & Design is a registered trademark of Penguin Random House LLC.
Printed in the USA.

Visit us online at www.penguinrandomhouse.com.

Library of Congress Control Number: 2016930739

ISBN 9780448488530   21 20 19 18 17 16 15
                                CW

Contents

Who Was Maya Angelou?

January 20, 1993, was a sunny and crisp winter day in Washington, DC. Maya Angelou, a six-foot-tall, sixty-four-year-old African American woman, stood on the steps of the Capitol Building. She wore a black coat, bright red lipstick, and gold hoop earrings. It was the day that America's forty-second president, William Jefferson Clinton, was taking office.

Maya was about to read her poem "On the Pulse of Morning" in front of two hundred fifty thousand people. Millions more watched on their televisions at home. It had been thirty-two years since a poem had been read at a presidential inauguration. She was the first African American and the first woman ever to do so. Despite being a prizewinning writer, she felt nervous.

"I tried not to realize where I was," she said later.

The crowd became silent and spellbound. She spoke powerfully in a deep voice that rose up and down like ocean waves as she read each line of her poem. The words called for peace and friendship between people around the world.

It took her six minutes to read the entire poem.
The last lines are:

> And say simply
> Very simply
> With hope—
> Good morning.

When Maya finished, the large crowd rose to its feet and broke into loud applause. President Clinton gave her a giant hug in thanks for her beautiful words.

Maya Angelou was a world-famous poet and writer. She was also a teacher, a civil rights champion, and a singer and dancer. And when she spoke, she had a beautiful and strong voice that was uniquely Maya's.

Through her ideas and words, Maya taught people to live with love and to treat one another with respect and kindness. Bringing joy to others, especially if they were down or sad, was very important. "Try to be a rainbow in someone's cloud," she said.

Despite a tough childhood, Maya used her voice. She became a rainbow for the whole world to see.

CHAPTER 1
Momma

Maya Angelou was born Marguerite Annie Johnson on April 4, 1928, in St. Louis, Missouri. Her mother, Vivian Baxter, was a nurse and also worked as a card dealer in a casino. Her father, Bailey Johnson, was a doorman at an apartment building. Vivian and Bailey already had a one-year-old son, Bailey Jr., when Maya was born.

Bailey Jr. couldn't say *Marguerite*, and called her "My-a Sister" instead. Soon, he began to just call her Maya. The nickname stuck.

Maya's mom and dad did not always get along, and their marriage was not easy. They had divorced by the time Maya was three years old. Neither parent thought they could take care of their children on their own. So Bailey Jr. and Maya were put on a train heading to Stamps, Arkansas, to stay with their grandmother.

KANSAS CITY

ST LOUIS

MISSISSIPPI RIVER

MISSOURI

ARKANSAS

LITTLE ROCK

STAMPS

Annie "Momma" Henderson was their father's mother. Bailey and Maya traveled alone. They had tags pinned to their shirtsleeves explaining who they were and where they were heading. Fellow passengers felt bad for the two young children— only three and four years old—sitting all alone.

They gave them "cold fried chicken and potato salad," Maya remembered.

Once Bailey and Maya arrived in Stamps, they moved in with Momma Henderson and her son, their uncle Willie. Stamps was a segregated town, and Momma owned a small general store in the black neighborhood. For the next four years, they lived in a few small rooms in the back of the store.

Segregation

Segregation is a system that keeps groups of people separated from each other. In the Southern United States until the 1960s, black people were kept apart from white people by Jim Crow laws. Under these rules, black children and white children went to separate schools.

Black people had to live in separate neighborhoods, eat at separate restaurants, and even drink from different water fountains and sit in different sections of movie theaters. They had to sit at the back of buses, while white people sat in front.

In 1964 and 1965, the US Congress passed laws— like the Civil Rights Act and the Voting Rights Act— that made this illegal.

LINE

Momma was a strict but loving woman. She insisted that Bailey and Maya use good manners, go to church every Sunday, and help out in the store. Maya swept the floor and even helped serve the customers lunch. Momma also insisted Maya and Bailey keep themselves very clean.

"Each night in the bitterest winter . . . we would go to the well and wash in the ice-cold, clear water," Maya said.

Uncle Willie insisted his niece and nephew develop their minds. He encouraged them to memorize the multiplication tables and to read as many books as they could. Momma also praised her grandchildren for studying hard. She sometimes called Maya her "little professor."

Thanks to Uncle Willie and Momma, Maya fell in love with words. Her favorite writer

was William Shakespeare. But all writers were
her friends, she said.

Throughout these four years in Stamps,
Bailey was Maya's real best friend. They
spent almost all their free time together
playing games like hide-and-seek and
follow the leader. He would sneak pickles
out of the jar in the store and always
share one with Maya.

Maya was a big girl with darker
skin than her brother and
hair like "black steel wool."
Sometimes adults told Maya
that she was unattractive and said
other unkind things about her
looks. Bailey always stood up for
his sister and made her feel better.
This made Maya love him even more.
"Bailey was the greatest person in my
world," she said.

CHAPTER 2
A Child with No Voice

One morning in 1935, Maya's father showed up in Stamps. He came to visit his children and stayed for three weeks. Then he took Bailey Jr. and Maya with him back to St. Louis, Missouri, to see their mother.

St. Louis was a lot different from tiny, rural Stamps, Arkansas. It was a big city with tall buildings and paved streets. Maya said it felt like a "foreign country" to her. She couldn't get used to all the loud city noises.

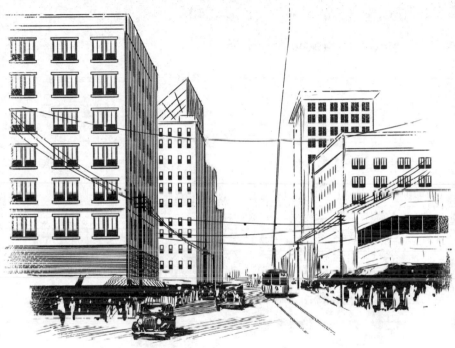

At first, Maya and Bailey lived in a big house with Vivian, their Grandmother Baxter, and their three uncles: Tutti, Tom, and Ira. Maya's mother was a beautiful woman who wasn't home very much. The times Bailey and Maya did see her were when she met them at a local tavern. Vivian danced to songs playing on the jukebox.

"I loved her most at those times," said Maya about her mother. "She was like a pretty kite that floated just above my head."

At school, Maya and Bailey were the best students because they had done so much reading and studying in Stamps. Maya spent her Saturdays at the local library. She loved having the whole day to read without any interruptions.

"Libraries and books said, 'Here I am, read me,'" Maya recalled.

After about six months, Vivian and the children moved in with Vivian's boyfriend, whom they called Mr. Freeman.

One day, when no one else was home, Mr. Freeman hurt Maya in a terrible way. He touched parts of her body that were private. Maya was only seven years old. She was hurt so badly that she stayed in bed for several days. The only person she told was her brother. Bailey cried for his sister. Then he told their mother, and Vivian went to the police. Mr. Freeman was arrested for what he did. But he was released from jail after just one day. A few days after that, a policeman came to Maya's door. He told the family that Mr. Freeman had been found dead. Someone had murdered him.

Maya couldn't believe it. She felt that Mr. Freeman must have died because she'd told Bailey what had happened. Maya was too young to understand that she hadn't done anything wrong. In fact, she had done the right thing by telling Bailey how Mr. Freeman had hurt her. But in her mind, Maya thought her words had killed Mr. Freeman. Maya decided to stop talking. She didn't want anyone to get hurt again. Maya would not speak in school, to her mother, her grandmother, or uncles. She would not even talk to Bailey! Vivian became frustrated with her daughter's silence. She didn't understand how sad and scared Maya was. She and Bailey were sent back to Stamps.

Maya didn't speak to anyone for the next
five years. Bailey did enough talking for both of
them. He made up funny stories about what their
life had been like in St. Louis. He told people,

"They've got watermelon twice the size of a cow's head and sweeter than syrup."

For her part, Maya kept journals of her thoughts and feelings. She fell in love with poetry and became even more interested in reading and writing. She thought of herself "as a giant ear which could just absorb all sound."

"I would go into a room and just eat up the sound," she said. "I memorized so many poets."

Finally, a close family friend in Stamps—a well-educated woman name Bertha Flowers—helped Maya rediscover her voice. One day, Bertha invited Maya back to her house and read to her part of the novel *A Tale of Two Cities*. It was by the famous writer Charles Dickens. Maya had already read the book, but she couldn't believe how beautiful the words sounded out loud. Maya thought Bertha's reading sounded like singing.

Charles Dickens (1812–1870)

Charles Dickens was one of the most popular English authors of the nineteenth century. Over the course of his lifetime he wrote fifteen novels and hundreds of short stories.

Much of Dickens's writing focuses on the difficult lives of poor people. The novel *Oliver Twist* exposed the terrible treatment of orphans in London, England, during his own lifetime.

His most famous works include *Great Expectations*, *A Tale of Two Cities*, and *A Christmas Carol*.

Charles Dickens is buried in Poets' Corner at Westminster Abbey—the site of royal weddings, coronations, and burials since 1066—in recognition of his contributions to British culture.

"Words mean more than what is set down on paper," Bertha explained to Maya. "It takes the human voice to infuse them with the shades of deeper meaning."

Maya took what Bertha said to heart. She soon began talking again by reading poems and books to Bertha. When Maya graduated from eighth grade at Lafayette County Training School in 1940, she had finally begun to speak again.

CHAPTER 3
The California Years

In 1941, Momma made up her mind that it was time for Maya and Bailey to live with Vivian, who had moved to San Francisco, California.

She thought they would have a chance to attend better schools on the West Coast. White people in Stamps still did not treat black people fairly. She thought Bailey and Maya would be safer in California.

Maya and Bailey, now thirteen and fourteen, enjoyed living in San Francisco. They loved living near the San Francisco Bay. They loved the Golden Gate Bridge and the red cable cars that went up and down the hills of the city streets.

Maya continued to do well in high school. She tried out for a dance and drama program and won a scholarship to attend evening classes at a local college.

In her free time, Maya read and wrote her own poetry and short stories. Vivian was now remarried to a man the children called Daddy Clidell, a successful businessman. Daddy Clidell was a loving and generous man, and Maya and Bailey thought of him as a father. Their real father, Bailey Sr., now lived in California, as well. He came to visit them sometimes. And once, he even took Maya on a trip to Mexico.

As Maya and Bailey grew up, Bailey lost interest in school. He started to hang around troublemakers who didn't like to study and sometimes skipped school. He began fighting with Vivian, too. Bailey did not like to be told what time to come home or what to do. After one really big fight, he ran away from home.

Maya was crushed when Bailey left. She began to have trouble with her schoolwork. She couldn't concentrate on her studies because she missed Bailey so much.

Maya decided to take some time off from high school and look for a job. After months of showing up at the railway offices begging for work, Maya was hired as a cable-car conductor!

She became the first African American conductor in the city of San Francisco. Maya was only fifteen years old.

San Francisco's Cable Cars

Invented in 1873, cable cars look like trains that run on mechanical railways throughout the streets of San Francisco. Close to seven million people ride the cars every year. Although some people use them to commute back and forth to work, many of today's riders are tourists visiting the city. Of the twenty-three original lines, only three still run today.

Maya worked as a cable-car conductor for one whole semester. Then she realized how important it was to go back to school. After Bailey ran away, he joined the US Merchant Marine—a fleet of ships that assist the navy. He began to write letters to his sister. Maya was thrilled to be in touch with her brother again.

Maya did well in high school. But during her senior year, she became pregnant. Still, she managed to stay in school, and in 1945, when she was seventeen, Maya graduated. Three weeks after that, Maya gave birth to a baby boy, Clyde Bailey Johnson. She called him Guy. Maya and the baby's father did not want to get married. She knew she had to take care of her son on her own.

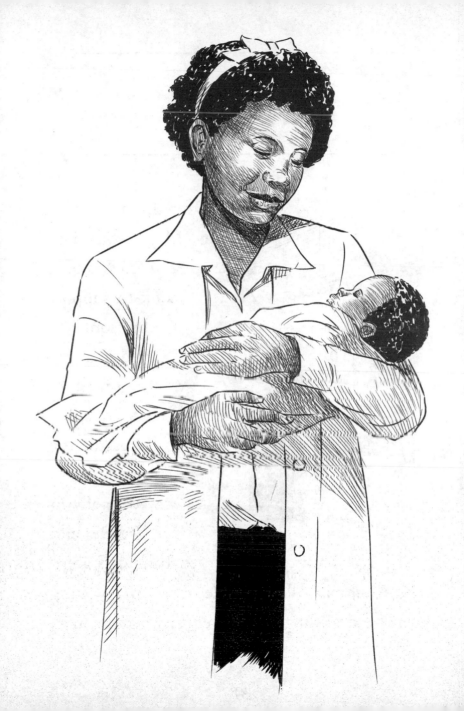

Chapter 4
A Big Break

Over the next seven years, Maya worked as a waitress and a cook to support her son. She lived in a tiny apartment in San Francisco most of the time, but also stayed briefly in Los Angeles and back in Stamps with Momma. All the while, Maya was writing poems and reading books every spare moment.

In 1950, when Maya was twenty-two years old, she got a job as a clerk in a music store. At work she met a sailor named Tosh Angelos.

Maya and Tosh both loved music. And Tosh loved to spend time with Guy. He taught him how to play chess and baseball.

Maya and Tosh married soon after meeting—but maybe too soon. It didn't take long for Maya to realize that she didn't have as much in common with Tosh as she'd thought. When they divorced, Maya decided to keep the last name Angelos. But she changed the last letter, from *s* to *u*. She liked how unique the name sounded. From now on, she would be known as Maya Angelou.

Maya no longer worked at the record store. She had begun working as a calypso dancer and singer at a popular San Francisco nightclub called the Purple Onion.

Maya had learned to dance during her high-school years. At first she was nervous to sing and dance onstage. She said, "My nerves shivered and the swallows in my stomach did nosedives." But once she began performing, she discovered she was a natural.

She was tall and her long legs were perfect

for dancing. And, although Maya never had any formal singing lessons, she had a naturally deep and soulful voice.

Calypso Music

Calypso is a type of music that began on the island country of Trinidad and Tobago in the nineteenth century. Slaves from West Africa had brought their kaiso music with them to the Caribbean islands centuries earlier. These rhythms eventually became the lively modern-day calypso.

One of the biggest calypso stars in history is the Trinidadian calyposonian Lord Kitchener. Born Aldwyn Roberts (1922–2000), Lord Kitchener became famous for hits such as "Green Fig" and "Jump in the Line."

In just a short time, Maya's performances became big news. Long lines of people formed outside the Purple Onion, waiting to see this dazzling woman. Sometimes, Maya even wrote her own songs, using the words from her poems.

Newspaper reporters began asking her for interviews. She even made guest appearances on radio and television shows.

One evening, some other professional performers came to see Maya dance and sing. They were from a company—a group of dancers and singers—touring and performing the musical *Porgy and Bess*.

The show is about African American life in the 1920s in Charleston, South Carolina.

One of the people in charge of the show was so impressed with Maya's performance that he invited her to try out for a part in *Porgy and Bess*. Maya did, and got the part. Maya's mother agreed to take care of Guy while Maya was away.

Although she was sad to leave Guy, now age nine, Maya felt like this was an opportunity she couldn't turn down. She joined the cast of *Porgy and Bess* on a twenty-two-nation tour across Europe and North Africa. They would perform on stages all over the world. Maya couldn't wait!

CHAPTER 5
Becoming a Writer

Maya loved seeing the world while touring with the cast of *Porgy and Bess*. They traveled to Canada, Italy, France, Egypt, and other parts of Africa. They performed in sold-out opera houses and received standing ovations. Maya discovered she was a natural at foreign languages, and learned to speak French and Italian. She loved to explore and learn about new cultures in every city she visited.

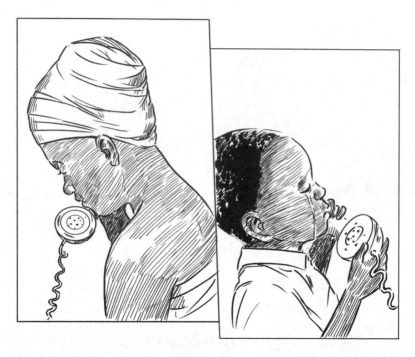

But Maya missed Guy terribly. When they spoke on the phone, the calls would end with both Maya and Guy in tears. After a year of traveling,

Maya received a letter from her mother. Guy had become sick. He had developed a severe rash all over his body. Doctors couldn't seem to heal it. Maya returned home to be with her son.

Back in San Francisco, Maya helped nurse her frail son back to health. She spent hours reading to him, taking him to the park, and cooking his favorite foods. She also made a promise to him that in the future, wherever she traveled, she would always bring him with her.

"I swear to you, I'll never leave you again," she told Guy. "If I go, when I go, you'll go with me or I won't go."

While she was helping Guy in San Francisco, Maya received some sad news about her beloved brother, Bailey. He was now in prison in New York for selling stolen goods.

For a time, Maya stayed in California and sang and danced at local nightclubs. In 1957,

she even had the chance to record an album called *Miss Calypso*. But Maya always felt like singing and dancing weren't her true calling.

Throughout the years, Maya had written many poems, and she had always kept a journal. She knew that she really wanted to be writer. She had lived through many hard times. But Maya had learned how to forgive and to love. She wanted to share these hopeful messages with others.

Maya and Guy were living in Los Angeles when she met John Oliver Killens, a famous writer from New York. John was in Los Angeles because one of his books was being made into a movie. He was writing the *screenplay*, or script, for the movie. Maya asked John to read some of her stories and poems. John thought Maya had a lot of talent. He encouraged her to move to New York City and join a group called the Harlem Writers Guild.

The Harlem Writers Guild

Harlem is a large neighborhood in New York City that has been a major center of artistic life and culture for the black American community since the early twentieth century.

The Harlem Writers Guild (HWG) was cofounded in 1950 by John Oliver Killens. Its original members met in a storefront in Harlem, and sometimes in John's home in Brooklyn. The HWG is the oldest organization of African American writers. Its most famous members include Terry McMillan, Walter Dean Myers, and Maya Angelou.

John Oliver Killens

When Maya first arrived in New York in 1959, she lived with John and his wife, Grace, until she was able to find a place where she and Guy could live on their own. Soon Maya found work as a singer in a nightclub. The singing job paid the rent and kept her days free to write.

"At first I limited myself to short sketches [descriptions]," said Maya about her writing, "then to song lyrics, then I dared short stories."

Maya also wrote plays and poetry. When Maya first read a play she wrote called *One Love. One Life.* at a Harlem Writers Guild meeting, she was so nervous her hands were sweaty and her tongue felt too big for her mouth. Once she finished the reading, she waited. Everyone in the group told her that her writing was terrible!

Maya was so hurt and angry. When John Clarke, another member of the group, spoke to Maya afterward, he said, "In this group, we remind each other that talent is not enough. You've got to work."

Maya took his words to heart. She wanted to be a good writer, and now she knew that she would have to work hard to make it happen.

CHAPTER 6
Civil Rights Activist

One day in 1960, Maya and a friend, Godfrey Cambridge, an actor and comedian, went to listen to Dr. Martin Luther King Jr. speak at a church in Harlem. Maya was inspired by Dr. King's words of peace and equal rights for everybody,

no matter the color skin of their skin. Maya and Godfrey decided to put on a show to raise money for Dr. King and his group, the Southern Christian Leadership Conference (SCLC). The group worked toward gaining civil rights for black people in America.

What Are Civil Rights?

Civil rights are the freedoms granted to citizens by their government. In the United States, these rights are guaranteed and protected by the Constitution. They include the freedom of speech, the right to vote, and the right to worship any religion. These rights are spelled out in a written statement called the Bill of Rights, which is part of the Constitution.

When slavery was abolished after the Civil War, black people were denied their civil rights, including the right to vote. They were segregated in the

poorest schools and offered only low-paying jobs.

Beginning in the 1950s, there was a national movement to end segregation and discrimination. The civil rights movement for black Americans was led by a young minister named Dr. Martin Luther King Jr. Through nonviolent protest actions, such as sitting at counters in white-only restaurants where they weren't welcome, civil rights activists eventually changed the laws in the United States to include *all* of its citizens.

Maya and Godfrey called their show Cabaret for Freedom, and it featured black singers and dancers at a jazz club in New York City. The show was a smashing success on opening night and continued to be a big hit for five straight weeks. The ticket sales of the show helped raised nine thousand dollars for Dr. King's cause.

Dr. King's group, the SCLC, asked Maya to become their regional coordinator. Maya happily accepted the job. Her duties included fund-raising, organizing volunteers, and speaking on behalf of the SCLC. After two months, she met Dr. King for the first time. He thanked her for all her hard work. Around this same time, Maya had her first short story published. It appeared in a Cuban magazine called *Revolucíon*.

"That it would appear only in Cuba, and probably in Spanish, did not dilute the fact that I was joining the elite group of published writers," Maya said.

In 1960, Maya met a man from South Africa named Vusumzi "Vus" Make at a dinner party in New York. At the time, South Africa had a white-run government that did not give black people in the country any rights. Just like Martin Luther King Jr. fought for the rights of black people in America, Vus fought for the rights of black people in South Africa.

Vusumzi Make

Vus was in the United States to speak to the United Nations—an organization of countries that fights for peace and human rights around the world—about his country's racial policy.

Maya and Vus hit it off instantly. They soon moved in together. Vus continued to travel and speak about human rights around the world.

Maya stopped working for the SCLC. Instead, she and a friend formed a new organization called the Cultural Association for Women of African Heritage (CAWAH). This organization worked to support human rights in both the United States and in South Africa. While working for CAWAH, Maya met another famous civil rights leader, Malcolm X.

Although Maya had met Malcolm X only briefly, she was in awe of his energy and commitment to the civil rights movement. He believed that black people should show pride in themselves and their African heritage.

After living together in New York for less than a year, Vus asked Maya to move with him to Cairo, Egypt. He planned to meet and work there with *freedom fighters*—those who were working hard to gain independence for their countries—from other African nations. Maya was always eager for a new adventure. She was ready to leave the United States again, but this time, just as she had promised years ago, she would bring Guy with her.

Malcolm X (1925–1965)

Malcolm X was born Malcolm Little in Omaha, Nebraska. He became one of the most important black civil rights leaders in American history.

Growing up, Malcolm was a bright student, but he dropped out of school. He became involved with drugs and stealing, and served seven years in jail for robbery. While in jail, Malcolm converted to the Islam religion. After being released in 1952, Malcolm joined the Nation of Islam, a Muslim religious and civil rights group. He changed his last name to X because he believed *Little* was a slave name. He became a powerful speaker and believed black people deserved to get equal rights "by any means necessary"——including violent ones. Malcolm's beliefs were in strong contrast to Martin Luther King Jr.'s ideas of peaceful resistance.

By the mid-1960s, Malcolm had changed his mind. He came to believe that equal rights for black people could be achieved through peaceful protest——not violence. He had doubts about the Nation of Islam's leadership and left them to start the Organization of Afro-American Unity. On February 21, 1965, Malcolm was shot and killed by three members of the Nation of Islam in New York City. He was only thirty-nine years old.

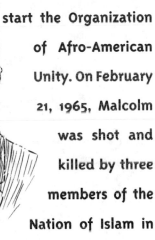

CHAPTER 7
Home Away From Home

When Maya and Guy arrived in Cairo in 1961, the streets and sidewalks were filled with cars, people . . . and goats, mules, and camels.

Maya asked their driver if it was a holiday. The driver answered her, "No, this is just everyday Cairo!" Maya and Guy loved all this excitement. They also came to realize that people, no matter what country they live in, aren't so very different. "Peoples cry, laugh, eat, worry, and die," Maya later wrote. "If we try to understand each other, we may even become friends."

Vus had rented a lovely furnished apartment for his family in Cairo. Fifteen-year-old Guy began high school just minutes outside of the city. Maya spent her days with Vus, meeting and talking with freedom fighters and other people from countries like Uganda and Kenya. A couple of months after moving to Egypt, Maya got a job as an editor for an English-language magazine called the *Arab Observer*. She wrote and edited stories about events happening all over the African continent.

Maya worked at the magazine for over a year. By then, Guy was ready to start college. He chose to attend the University of Ghana in West Africa. Maya decided to go with Guy and live in the city of Accra while he was in school. Vus stayed behind in Cairo.

CAIRO

EGYPT

GHANA

SOUTH
AFRICA

When Maya and Guy arrived in Ghana, they immediately felt like they belonged there. Ghana was an independent African country. In 1957, it had been the first African country in the region to break free from its ruling power, Great Britain. By 1962, all Ghana's black people were being treated equally, unlike in the United States and other countries around the world.

One night shortly after they arrived, Guy was in a terrible car accident. His neck was broken in three places, and his arm and leg were fractured.

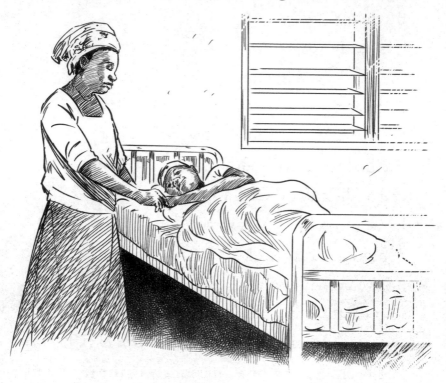

For the next two months, Guy stayed in the hospital. Maya visited her son every day. Guy eventually recovered and was finally able to begin his studies at the University of Ghana. Maya found a job as an office assistant at the university. This way, she could care for her son, who was still recovering. Maya also began to write for the newspaper the *Ghanaian Times*. She reconnected with friends she had known from the Harlem Writers Guild who had since moved to Ghana. Their names were Julian Mayfield and Dr. Ana Livia Cordero, his wife.

One night, Julian and Ana invited Maya to a dinner party, where Maya had the chance to see Malcolm X again. Before traveling back to the United States, he had stopped to see his old friends.

After Malcolm returned to New York, he wrote letters to Maya back in Ghana. Malcolm had remembered the work Maya had done for Dr. King, as well as for the Cultural Association for Women of African Heritage. In one of his letters, Malcolm asked Maya if she would consider coming back to New York to work for a group he had founded, the Organization of Afro-American Unity (OAAU).

Maya discussed it with Guy. They both decided this was something that was important for her to do. Guy, now nineteen, was also ready for more independence. He stayed in Ghana to continue his studies, and Maya headed back to America. It was February 1965, and Maya had been living abroad for four years. She was ready to return home.

CHAPTER 8
Becoming a Famous Writer

Maya, now age thirty-seven, decided to visit her mother and her brother, Bailey, before she started work in New York City. Maya flew from Ghana to San Francisco, where her mother still lived. Bailey was out of jail and working as a chef in Hawaii. He flew to California to see his mother and his sister.

The siblings had written each other over the years, but had not seen each other in a long time.

Maya spent the weekend reconnecting with her mom and brother. They talked and laughed. They shared happy memories from when Maya and Bailey were children. On February 21, 1965, a Sunday morning, Maya heard the terrible news that Malcolm X had been assassinated. He was shot and killed while speaking for the OAAU in Harlem.

Deeply saddened and with no reason to move back to New York, Maya went to Hawaii with Bailey. She worked as a nightclub singer for six months. Then Maya returned to California where Guy, now a college graduate, had come to live.

But shortly after her arrival, a truck slammed into Guy and the parked car he was sitting in. His neck was broken again. Maya visited her son every day. When Guy was finally on his way to a full recovery, Maya moved back to New York City to write with the Harlem Writers Guild again. She was determined to pursue her writing career.

Over the next couple of years in New York, Maya wrote two plays. She also worked on her poetry. One night, she went to see Martin Luther King Jr. speak at Carnegie Hall. Afterward, Maya and her friends met with Dr. King. He asked Maya if she would come and work for him again. This time, he asked her to travel around the country and ask churches to help support his cause. Maya agreed.

On April 4, 1968, Maya was getting ready to go to her fortieth birthday party. She was supposed to start working for Dr. King in the next few days. A friend rushed over to Maya's apartment and told her that Dr. King had been shot and killed in Memphis, Tennessee.

Maya was crushed by Dr. King's death and did not leave her apartment for weeks. Friends were afraid she would stop speaking again, just like she had when she was a young girl. Finally, James Baldwin, a friend from the Harlem Writers Guild, helped Maya break free of her sadness.

James Baldwin (1924–1987)

James Arthur Baldwin was an American novelist, essayist, and playwright who wrote on the subject of race in America.

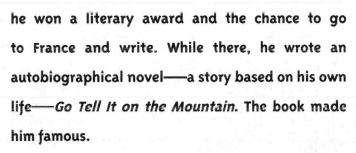

James was born in the Harlem neighborhood of New York City. In 1948, he won a literary award and the chance to go to France and write. While there, he wrote an autobiographical novel——a story based on his own life——*Go Tell It on the Mountain*. The book made him famous.

Later in his life, James returned to the United States and became involved in the civil rights movement. He published many essays, novels, and short stories about racial issues in America.

James Baldwin, along with other friends, encouraged Maya to write her own life story. They told her to share the stories of how she had survived so much pain and sorrow.

Maya took their advice. She decided to write her first autobiography. An *autobiography* is the true story of the writer's life. She called the book *I Know Why the Caged Bird Sings*. The title came from a famous line in the poem "Sympathy" by Paul Laurence Dunbar. The poem was about a bird that wanted its freedom. Maya used this title to mean she sometimes felt like a bird in a cage, too. She wanted to be free from "the cage" of abuse, racism, poverty, and cruelty.

The stories Maya told about her childhood were full of sadness, but also full of hope. Maya thought that no matter how hard life can be, people can survive and learn to be happy.

The book was published in 1969 and it became a best seller. Maya was now a famous writer.

CHAPTER 9
A Hero to Us All

Maya was living in New York when her first collection of poems, *Just Give Me a Cool Drink of Water 'fore I Diiie*, was published. It came out just two years after her best-selling autobiography. The thirty-eight poems express what it is like to be a black woman in the United States. Her poems were meant to be read out loud.

"I write for the voice, not the eye," she said.

Maya's poem "Harlem Hopscotch" addresses the hardships black children have faced over time.

One foot down, then hop! It's hot.
Good things for the ones that's got.
Another jump, now to the left.
Everybody for hisself.
In the air, now both feet down.
Since you black, don't stick around.
Food is gone, the rent is due,
Curse and cry and then jump two.

Just Give Me a Cool Drink of Water 'fore I Diiie was nominated for the Pulitzer Prize in 1972. In the United States, this award is one of the highest honors an author can receive. That same year, Maya became the first African American woman to have her own screenplay—the script for a movie—produced. The story, called *Georgia, Georgia*, was about a young black woman who falls in love with a white man. In addition to writing the screenplay, Maya wrote the music for the film, too!

Even though she was now very busy, Maya found time to star in a Broadway play called *Look Away*. In 1973, she received a Tony nomination—the highest award for US stage actors—for her performance.

Maya was now living the life of a famous author and writing as many as sixteen hours a day! She traveled a lot and attended fancy dinner parties. While visiting London, Maya met

Paul du Feu, a British writer and cartoonist. They soon fell in love and married. Maya was forty-five years old and world-famous. She and Paul moved to California just outside of San Francisco.

They both spent much of their time writing. Maya's son, Guy, was also married and had a son of his own named Colin. Guy and his family lived close to Maya and Paul.

In 1977, Maya had a role in a miniseries on television called *Roots*, a popular show about the history of American slavery. Maya received an Emmy nomination for playing a grandmother called Nyo Boto.

Roots

Roots is a television miniseries that first aired in 1977. It was based on the best-selling novel *Roots: The Saga of An American Family* by Alex Haley. The story follows Kunta Kinte and his family's journey——from his birth in West Africa in 1750, through Kunta's capture, to slavery, and finally to his descendants' freedom——  over a course of two hundred years.

More than 130 million Americans tuned in to watch *Roots*. This was more than half the population of the United States at the time. It is one of the most successful television miniseries of all time.

Roots received thirty-six Emmy nominations. The final show of the series was the third most-watched episode of television in American history.

In 1978, Maya's third book of poems, *And Still I Rise*, was published. It included one of Maya's most well-known poems, "Still I Rise."

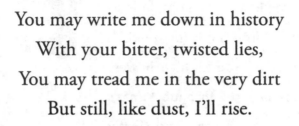

The poem began:

> You may write me down in history
> With your bitter, twisted lies,
> You may tread me in the very dirt
> But still, like dust, I'll rise.

In 1981, Maya and Paul divorced after eight years of marriage. Although they remained friends, they were both too busy to make life work as a couple.

During these years, Maya was also giving speeches and reading her poems at different universities across the country. She was a beloved author who had a kind word and genuine smile for everyone she met. In her speeches, she shared what she'd learned through her personal experiences. She spread her message of peace and unity.

"One can never know too many good people,"
Maya said. "I have learned that a friend may be
waiting behind a stranger's smile."

Maya soon accepted a position at Wake Forest University in Winston-Salem, North Carolina, as a professor of American studies. Most college professors have a doctorate or at least graduate degrees. But Maya had never even gone to college!

Maya continued to write in North Carolina while teaching students about history and poetry. Even without a college degree, Maya had plenty of life experience to share with her students. "I'm not a writer who teaches," she once said in an interview. "I'm a teacher who writes."

Maya continued to deliver countless lectures and poetry readings all over the country over the next thirty years. She spoke about the importance of forgiveness and the strength of the human spirit. People loved her strong, musical voice.

They respected her for surviving so many tough and disappointing times. She had never given up. She was not bitter. Instead, Maya was graceful and loving, and she poured her heart into her words and her work. People were inspired by her strength and spirit.

In 1993, Maya was honored to read her poem "On the Pulse of Morning" at the inauguration of President Bill Clinton.

Maya worked day and night writing the poem. Although the final poem was only sixty-seven words, she had filled more than two hundred handwritten pages with ideas before it was finally finished. The poem was instantly popular. It encouraged people to be hopeful about the future, no matter how bad the past has been.

President Clinton loved every word. He said, "She was without a voice for five years and then she developed the greatest voice on the planet." The famous poet Robert Frost had been the only other person to read a poem at an inauguration—and that had been over thirty years earlier.

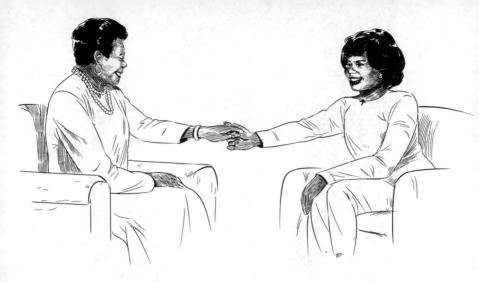

Over the years, Maya had developed a strong friendship with television host Oprah Winfrey. They called each other "mother-sister-friends" to express their closeness. Maya appeared on Oprah's popular television show countless times, which introduced her writing and her ideas to a huge television audience.

In 2000, Maya was awarded the National Medal of Arts. In 2005, she wrote the poem "Amazing Peace: A Christmas Poem" for President George W. Bush, and delivered the poem at that year's Christmas-tree-lighting ceremony.

In 2010, President Barack Obama presented her
with the Presidential Medal of Freedom. It is the
highest honor that a *civilian*—someone not in
the military—can receive. During the ceremony,

Maya's writing was described as teaching us "to reach across division and honor the beauty of our world."

Most importantly, Maya continued to teach people how every person can rise from tragedy and hardship to live a meaningful life. Her message had always been one of love, hope, and courage.

"I've learned that people will forget what you said, people will forget what you did, but people will never forget how you made them feel," she famously said.

On May 28, 2014, Maya Angelou died peacefully in her home in North Carolina. She was eighty-six years old. The US Postal Service honored Maya with her own stamp on April 7, 2015, less than a year after her death. On the stamp was a portrait of Maya, as well as one of her quotes: "A bird doesn't sing because it has an answer, it sings because it has a song."

Over the course of her lifetime, Maya published more than thirty books, including eleven autobiographies and fourteen books of poetry. She also wrote five children's books, including *Life Doesn't Frighten Me*, which was based on one of her poems. Most of her books were best sellers.

After she died, many celebrities and past US presidents spoke about what Maya and her work meant to them. Maya had befriended almost every important black leader, writer, and activist from Martin Luther King Jr. to President Barack Obama, and everyone wanted the chance to pay tribute.

A Celebration of Rising "Joy"!

DR. MAYA ANGELOU
APRIL 4, 1928 ~ MAY 28, 2014

"Maya was many things—an author, poet, civil rights activist, playwright, actress, director, composer, singer and dancer. But above all, she was a storyteller—and her greatest stories were true," said President Barack Obama. "A childhood of suffering and abuse actually drove her to stop speaking—but the voice she found helped generations of Americans find their rainbow amidst the clouds, and inspired the rest of us to be our best selves."

Timeline of Maya Angelou's Life

1928	Marguerite Annie "Maya" Johnson is born April 4 in St. Louis, Missouri
1931	Sent to Stamps, Arkansas, to live with her grandmother
1941	Moves to San Francisco, California, with her mother
1944	Hired as the first black streetcar conductor in San Francisco
1945	Son Clyde Bailey "Guy" Johnson is born
1953	Officially changes her name to Maya Angelou
1960	Works for Dr. Martin Luther King Jr. as a coordinator of the Southern Christian Leadership Conference
1969	First autobiography, *I Know Why the Caged Bird Sings*, is published
1972	First book of poetry, *Just Give Me a Cool Drink of Water 'fore I Diiie*, is nominated for the Pulitzer Prize
1977	Appears in the TV miniseries *Roots*
1982	Becomes a professor at Wake Forest University
1993	Reads her poem "On the Pulse of Morning," at President Clinton's first inauguration on January 20
2000	Awarded the National Medal of Arts
2008	Celebrates her eightieth birthday on April 4 Publishes the book *Letter to My Daughter*
2010	Receives the Presidential Medal of Freedom, the country's highest civilian honor
2014	Dies on May 28 in Winston-Salem, North Carolina

Timeline of the World

Amelia Earhart becomes first woman to fly across the Atlantic	1928
"The Star-Spangled Banner" officially becomes the national anthem of the United States	1931
The first McDonald's hamburger stand opens in San Bernardino, California	1940
Jackie Robinson joins the Brooklyn Dodgers, becoming the first African American in modern times to play Major League Baseball	1947
The Supreme Court declares that schools can no longer be segregated	1954
Rosa Parks is arrested for refusing to give her seat to a white passenger on a bus in Montgomery, Alabama	1955
90 percent of all homes in the United States now own a television set	1960
Atari introduces *Pong*, one of the earliest and most popular video games ever	1972
Sandra Day O'Connor becomes the first woman on the US Supreme Court	1981
Terrorists attack the World Trade Center's Twin Towers in New York City and the Pentagon outside Washington, DC, on September 11	2001
Barack Obama takes office as the first African American president	2009

Bibliography

*Books for young readers

* Agins, Donna Brown. *Maya Angelou: A Biography of an Award-Winning Poet and Civil Rights Activist.* Berkeley Heights, NJ: Enslow, 2013.

Editors of Essence. *Maya Angelou: Her Phenomenal Life & Poetic Journey.* New York: Essence Books, 2014.

* Egan, Jill. *Maya Angelou: A Creative and Courageous Voice.* Pleasantville, NY: Gareth Stevens, 2009.

* Nardo, Don. *Maya Angelou: Poet, Performer, Activist.* Minneapolis: Compass Point Books, 2009.

* Pettit, Jayne. *Maya Angelou: Journey of the Heart.* New York: The Penguin Group, 1998.

BOOKS BY MAYA ANGELOU

The Collected Autobiographies of Maya Angelou. New York: Random House, 2004.

The Complete Collected Poems of Maya Angelou. New York: Random House, 1994.

Letter to My Daughter. New York: Random House, 2008.

Mom & Me & Mom. New York: Random House, 2013.

Rainbow in the Cloud: The Wisdom and Spirit of Maya Angelou. New York: Random House, 2014.

WEBSITES

www.mayaangelou.com